Bygone Peebles
Alex F. Young

A Southern Milk Transport Company's Albion lorry on its daily round collecting milk from farms in the Peebles area in the late 1930s. Alexander Wight ran the business from his home at Hampden Cottage, Carlops, before renting Langside Farm, on Edinburgh Road, Peebles, as a depot. He died of heart disease, aged 61 years, in December 1934, whilst delivering milk on Edinburgh's Princes Street, and was buried at Kelso Cemetery. He was succeeded by his 26 year old son William Fairbairn Wight, then a motor salesman on Orkney who had married Olivia Peterina Clouston at Stromness, the previous year. In 1936 William registered the company, with himself as the sole subscriber, holding 15,000 of the £1 shares. It is uncertain when he relinquished the business, but he died at Alwoodley, Leeds on 13th October 1972.

Part of the congregation of over 300 at the annual commemorative service, conducted by the Rev John W Murray, at St. Gordian's Cross, Manor Parish on Sunday, 5th July 1908. At the evening service in Manor Parish Church the dedication of a new organ filled the church to capacity. The cross, erected in 1874 by Sir John Murray Naesmyth (1804-1876) of Posso, bears the inscription; *Sacred to the memory of the Burnets of Burnetland and Barns, many generations of whom lie here interred. They were of Norman descent and were landed proprietors in Peeblesshire from about 1100 to 1838.* As St. Gordian's Church and graveyard, tradition tells of its use from Roman times – Gordian having been a Pro-Consul in Gaul, who was put to death for embracing Christianity – as a place of retreat for Christian soldiers who could worship unmolested. At a later period the Gordian Memorial Church was built, which survived until the Reformation of 1560. A new church, seating 150, was built at Kirkton, using stone from the Gordian Church, which was replaced by today's church building in 1874.

© Alex F. Young, 2022
First published in the United Kingdom, 2022,
by Stenlake Publishing Ltd.
www.stenlake.co.uk

ISBN 978-1-84033-940-6

The publishers regret that they cannot supply copies of any pictures featured in this book.

Printed by
Claro Print, Office 26, 27, 1 Spiersbridge Way,
Thornliebank, Glasgow G46 8NG

Acknowledgements

National Motor Museum Trust, Beaulieu, Hampshire, Wendy Purves, Douglas Whitie.

Further Reading

The following were the principal books and websites used by the author during his research. With the exception of *Old Peebles* none are available from Stenlake Publishing; please contact your local bookshop, reference library or search for them on the internet.

The Statistical Account of Scotland, Volume XII, County of Peebles, pub. William Creech, Edinburgh, 1794.
The New Statistical Account of Scotland, Volume III, County of Peebles, pub. William Blackwood & Sons, Edinburgh, 1834.
William Chambers, *A History of Peeblesshire*, pub. William and Robert Chambers, Edinburgh and London, 1864.
Francis H Groome, *Ordnance Gazetteer of Scotland*, Thos. C. Jack, Grange Publishing Works, Edinburgh, 1885.
Rev Alex Williamson, *Glimpses of Peebles*, pub George Lewis, Selkirk, 1895.
Rhona Wilson, *Old Peebles*, Stenlake Publishing Ltd, 1998.

Newspapers
The Era (1838-1939).
Peeblesshire Advertiser (1879-1892).
The Scots Magazine (1739-1900).
The Scotsman (1817-1950).
The Southern Reporter (1858-1945).
The Stage (1880-2007).

Introduction

The Royal Burgh of Peebles may have been granted its status in 1152 by King David I, for which there is no surviving charter, or in 1367 by King David II, for which there is. Despite the extra taxation through burgage tenure (a town rental property held by the monarch), the advantages of a crown charter included, parliamentary representation, and the commercial privileges in conducting foreign trade. A charter by Queen Mary, dated 17th December 1554, brought the liberty to hold markets and fairs. Tuesday was market day and there were five fairs in the year.

The earliest settlement was on the peninsula formed at the confluence of the Tweed and the Eddleston Water. The castle which stood here (the site of today's parish church) was captured by the English under King Edward I in 1301-1302, but re-taken by the Scots under King Robert I and demolished. The Cuddy Bridge over the Eddleston takes the road into today's Old Town. A sketch map of 1569, reproduced in William Chambers' book *A History of Peeblesshire* shows the Old Town, extending west to 'Nidpath' with the Old Market Place, the Hospitium of Abbot of Arbroath and St. Andrews Church. The castle looked up today's High Street (originally *Hie Gait*), the heart of the New Town, leading to East Port and Northgait, whilst the Port Brae (West Port) led down to the 15th century Tweed Bridge.

Peebles remained a royal burgh until, under the terms of the General Police and Improvement (Scotland) Act 1862, it became a police burgh, with a council consisting of a provost, two baillies, seven councillors, a dean of guild, a treasurer and a town clerk. The 'Commissioners of Police' first met on Thursday, 19th May 1864. When Peeblesshire County Council was created by the Local Government (Scotland) Act of 1889, Peebles sent three representatives. By 1901 'commissioners' were out of fashion and the town was governed by Peebles Town Council but only until 1975, when it became a small part of Borders Regional Council. In 1996 it was the same small part of Scottish Borders Council – as Tweeddale District.

Scotland's earliest census was conducted by the Rev Alexander Webster of Edinburgh – *An Account of the Number of People in Scotland in the Year One Thousand Seven Hundred and Fifty Five* – when the country's population amounted to 1,265,380. Of these, 1,896 lived in the Parish of Peebles, and of those, 379 were men of fighting age. Researching the *Statistical Account* for the parish in 1791 (pub. 1794), the Rev William Dalgleish found the figures to be: Old Town, 350; New Town, 1,130 (total 1,480); Landward, 440. He also records that – *Lately there were 6 men living at the same time, within fifty yards of one another, in the old town of Peebles, whose ages together amounted to 518 years, and who, several of them, died near 100 years old.* The population figure for 2021 is approximately 8,940.

As 1819 closed and the new year opened, the Scottish lawyer Henry Thomas Cockburn (1779-1854) – later Solicitor General and High Court Judge – was in Edinburgh. The 'Scottish Insurrection' or 'Radical War', a period of unrest following the Napoleonic Wars, was raging across the country – and would lead to the execution of James Wilson at Glasgow and John Baird and Andrew Hardie at Stirling, all for Treason. However, such was the peace in the city on Hogmanay, that Cockburn entered in his diary (published as *Memorials of His Time*, 1856), *Edinburgh was as quiet as the grave, or even as Peebles*.

The opening of the railway line to Edinburgh in 1855, brought Peebles out of its isolation. The mills benefitted through the cheaper transportation of raw materials and coal and, the sale of finished products. It also brought visitors, to the benefit of the Commercial Hotel, the Tontine and the Crown Hotel on High Street, the Cross Keys on Northgate and the Railway Hotel on Old Town. For the week ending 25th July 1857 the Peebles Railway carried 2,661 passengers, many of whom would have been day-trippers, coming and going. It was the start of Peebles as a resort. As such, later promotions for the town latched onto the phrase, *Peebles for Pleasure*, but where had it come from? In 1874, The Edinburgh Publishing Co, published the *Book of Scottish Anecdotes*, edited by Alexander Hislop, one of which runs; *An honest old citizen of Peebles was enabled by some strange chance to visit Paris. When he returned he was eagerly questioned as to the character of the French capital, to which he answered that – "Paris, a' thing considered, was a wonderfu' place; but still, gie me Peebles for pleasure!"*

The opening of the 120 bed 'Hydro' in July 1881, helped the railway – and Peebles. As commuters into Edinburgh were recognised as having long term value, the *Edinburgh Evening Courant* of 16th June 1857 carried the advertisement; *The DIRECTORS of the PEEBLES RAILWAY COMPANY, to induce parties to erect Dwelling-Houses in the vicinity of Peebles, will grant a FREE TICKET for a Term of Years to the Principal Occupant of each House, of a certain value.*

The 1856 Ordnance Survey map shows the town concentrated around High Street, Eastgate and Northgate, with a ribbon development along Old Town. Young Street led to an unnamed country road, soon to be Rosetta Road. The road south from Tweed Bridge forked. The left led onto Bridge-end (later Kingsmeadows Road), and the right, past Hayston Place, would become Springhill Road. From the 1920s this area would see more and more housing developments – PEEBLES. SPRINGHILL ROAD – *For Sale, New Villas. Substantial Semi-detached Stone built Front, with 2 Public, 4 Bed Rooms, Bath. Garden back and front. Ground reserved for Garage. Apply for particulars to Thos. Murray, Joiner, Peebles.* (*The Scotsman*, 14th March 1925).

The railway is gone and the mills are a memory, but Peebles thrives as a commuter town and attractive tourist centre.

High Street, looking west to the Parish Church, in the 1930s from the Chambers Institute on the left. On the right, as part of Veitch's building, was the bookseller and stationer David Clark and the hairdresser, Andrew Gordon Wemyss.

The shops at 19 to 25 High Street were built with the Carnegie Library above, and leased by the Public Library Committee. At No. 19 was Thomas Spalding (1847-1927), a nurseryman of Cairnswood, Innerleithen Road; Johnston's Dairy, Nellie Johnston of 65 Northgate; her neighbour was Edinburgh born Jasper Aikman, a chiropodist and barber who, in 1907 was advertising his services as a chiropodist, hair and scalp specialist at Maxwell's Hotel, Galashiels. He died in Edinburgh Royal Infirmary in March 1919, aged 43 years. To the right was Thomas Hush, the grocer and wine merchant who, in April 1912, was granted a liquor licence for this new premises. The 'Lion's Head' drinking fountain at the roadside was manufactured by Glenfield & Kennedy of Kilmarnock, Ayrshire, and may have been one of the two gifted to the town by Sir Adam Hay of Haystoun House in 1859. At least one fountain survives, painted red, at the entrance to Tweed Green Park opposite School Brae.

Supporters of Peebles Rovers Football Club in the quadrangle of the Chambers Institute on the evening of Thursday, 20th June 1907, for a fundraising fancy dress cycle parade. The town council granted permission for the event, and had a constable – on the left, above the umbrella – attend, to ensure the entrance to the Institute Library was not obstructed. Much of the courtyard was lost to the War Memorial (unveiled 5th October 1922 by Field Marshall Earl Haig) and its garden. The photograph is by Charles Steedman Kerr of Northgate, who took over the editorship of the 1887 founded *Peebles News* on the death of his father James Alexander Kerr, of Priorsford Villa, in 1908. For health reasons he emigrated to Auckland, New Zealand, in 1920, where he died in March 1932.

Peebles Rovers Football Club at Edinburgh's Tynecastle Park (home to Heart of Midlothian Football Club) on Saturday, 16th March 1912, after beating Broxburn Athletic 2 – 1 in the final of the East of Scotland Qualifying Cup, having beaten Coldstream 2-0 in the semi-final. At Tynecastle, the Rovers fielded: Macpherson; McLean and Wilson; Bain (scored, penalty), "Sanderson" and Mulholland; Macdonald (scored) (signed the previous week from Alloa Athletic), Curran, Buchan, Elder and Boylan. Of the crowd of 1,000, six hundred were from Peebles, having travelled by special train – *for which they had to provide their own coal*. Founded in 1893, the Rovers played at Victoria Park on Kingsmeadows Road until 1906, when they joined the cricket club on the council owned Whitestone Park (2022; The Gyles Leisure Centre and Playing Fields). In 1935 a 500 seat stand, with an enclosure for 300, was built, the footballers paid a rental of £45 for each nine month season.

A detachment of the Royal Scots marching along Eastgate, from Northgate, to their training camp at Kingsmeadows Park in May, 1915. The white two-storey, building to the left, on the Eastgate – Tweedbrae (previously The Vennel) corner, and opposite the 1872 built Free Church, was The Priory, occupied by Thomas Henderson Orphoot (1833-1917), Sheriff Substitute for Peeblesshire. Dating from the 18th century, it was known as Quebec Hall from the occupancy of Francis Russell (d. 1798), a one time Director of the Military Hospital at Quebec, Canada. From the mid-1850s John Thomson, plumber and, for a time, agent for the *Peeblesshire Advertiser* newspaper, owned the property, which he let to Orphoot, who bought it in the late 1870s. In 1920 it was purchased from Orphoot's estate by Andrew Miller Robertson, a retired Assistant Keeper of Sasines at Edinburgh, who died in the house in March 1937. The following year it was bought by the Post Master General for a new post office and telephone exchange.

The crowds on High Street on Midsummer Day, Friday, 21st June 1907, for the opening of Peebles March Riding ceremony and the crowning of the Beltane Queen on the steps of the Parish Church, at 10.30am. Supported by 400 children, 13 year old Jessie McLauchlan Taylor, daughter of power loom tuner William Taylor, 73 Rosetta Road, and dux of Kingsland School, was crowned by Mrs A O Murray, wife of the Master of Elibank, and presented with a commemorative gold bracelet. In 1918, whilst a teacher, she married Robert Sharp, a Glasgow bank clerk, then serving as a private in the Territorial Army Medical Corps. Of the shops featured, on the north side of High Street, the clothier Cooper & Dalling is now (2022) the restaurant *Prince of India* and John Mill, Clothier is now the estate agent *Walker Scott Ireland*.

It is shortly after 1.00pm and the 1907 March Riding is breaking up on Eastgate, having fulfilled its annual duty. Taken from the plinth of the Old Market Cross, the photograph is flanked by Miss Margaret Spalding's fancy goods shop on the left and St. Peter's Episcopal Church (built 1833-36) and Quebec Hall, on the right. That year's Cornet was 42 year old wood merchant William Yellowlees of Craigsford Cottage, 15 Cross Street, where he died on 5th December 1912, aged 48 years, with his henchmen, Charles Runciman of Eastgate and William J F Milne of Elderscroft.

May Alice Armstrong, the Beltane Queen of 1935, *by virtue of her educational attainments at Kingsland School*, at the entrance to the Chambers Institution, with her attendants and the Maharajah Kumar Sahib of Sant, India, who had gifted a silver shield to the March Riding Committee for the annual sports. Thirteen year old May was the daughter of James Armstrong, a railway porter of Old Railway Station Cottages, March Street. On 24th July 1942 she married George Adam Robson, a constable with Peeblesshire Constabulary, stationed at Peebles.

Old Town around 1906 with the 1888 built Peebles Co-operative Society shop on the left and the West United Presbyterian Church, on Elcho Street Brae corner, to the right. The foundation stone of the red sandstone church was laid in September 1891, on a site named Blinkbonny, and completed in March 1893, at a cost of £4,000. The internal woodwork, including the pulpit and the pews, were of New Zealand grown Kauri timber, gifted by Alexander Richardson Watson (1828-1911) of the Auckland Timber Company, and native of Peebles. In 1976 the congregation (St. Andrews from 1918) joined the Leckie Memorial Church and sold this site to the Ark Housing Association which, having demolished the church, built the social housing of St. Andrews Court – opened January 1983 by Mrs Judy Steel. The first tenement beyond the church was owned by Mrs Marion Mitchell of Crossland Crescent and let to Robert Watson of South Park Farm who operated the Bonnington Dairy from here. This was part of the A72 trunk road – from Galashiels to Hamilton – running through Peebles' Innerleithen Road, High Street, Cuddy Bridge and out along Old Town, and hence the responsibility of Peeblesshire County Council's Roads Committee. The narrowness of Old Town was a problem, but was overcome by moving the church entrance, and demolishing the buildings, on the north side, from the church to No. 34, which was completed by August 1938.

The 1888 built Peebles Co-operative Store Company's building on the Greenside Place – Old Town junction in the 1920s, previously their bakery. Founded in November 1875 with a capital balance of £99 10s 5d, and premises on the north side of High Street, its first half year turnover was £254.18/-, giving a dividend of £6.10/-. By the time of this photograph, quarterly sales were £19,313 10s 1d to a membership of 1,200. The foundation stone was laid by the company's president, William Broadhead, on 30th June 1888, and working to plans by local architect, Robert Murray, the builders Wilkie & Graham of Damdale had the building ready for opening in February 1889. The accommodation comprised of a provision shop, measuring 37ft by 35ft, with cellar, a bread shop (19ft by 13ft) and a wide passage at the rear for deliveries. The first floor held committee rooms and a showroom, with more storerooms on the top floor. In 1968 Peebles amalgamated with Galashiels United and Innerleithen to form the Border Co-operative Society. On 26th October 1918, Broadhead died of Spanish Flu in his home at 18 Biggiesknowe, rented from the Public Library Committee it having been the birthplace of William (1800) and Robert (1802) Chambers, founders of the town's museum and art gallery.

Early 20th century Northgate, looking north to Venlaw House on the hill above the trees. On Bridgegate corner, on the left, is the licensed grocer Alexander Irvine (d.1929), who had succeeded Alexander Thomson, also a grocer, who had died in 1887. The 1856 Ordnance Survey map (XIII.6) of Peebles shows the building as 'residence of Mungo Park, 1801-02'. Park (1771-1806), famed for his explorations in West Africa, had his surgery at 5 High Street, which was demolished and re-built in 1887, with an inscribed stone. Back in Northgate, the grocer's neighbour was the 1772 built masonic lodge (Lodge Peebles Kilwinning No. 24) marked on the 1856 map as *Freemason's Tavern and Freemason's Lodge*. On the right of the photograph, the barber's pole was on the premises of the Aberdeen born hairdresser William Swanson (1847-1913).

The post office on the Northgate – Ushers Wynd Corner, shortly after its opening on Monday, 16th May 1904, having left a post box at its previous premises, 45 High Street (2022, William Purves, funeral director). In the late 1890s the General Post Office bought the three house building at 37, 37a, and 39 Northgate from Peebles Kilwinning No. 24 Freemasons Society, its owner since 1771, and in April 1903 granted the £2,300 contract for the demolition of the houses and the erection of the post office, to local builder William Tod (1857-1922). Work commenced immediately. In their edition of 26th September 1903, the *Edinburgh Evening News* reported that the work was making rapid progress, *and will prove an ornament to the Northgate*. The move from High Street to Northgate, a less central position, was due to an increase in the volume of letters handled – from 11,100 per week in 1891 to 24,200 in 1902 – and hence the need for a larger premises. Postmaster Donald M'Intyre oversaw the move and remained in Peebles until Andrew Mercer took over in 1909. Tod the builder's immediate future was bleak. In December 1905 his business went into liquidation and in May 1906, his 50 year old wife Agnes died of heart failure in their home at 14 Damdale, Peebles.

Sheep graze on Ninian's Haugh by the river, with the Tweed Bridge leading to the Parish Church, the Tweedside Inn and Port Brae on the north bank. Victoria Park, Tweed Green, Cuddy Green and Ninian's Haugh were common property of the town and let annually, at a roup, or auction, for grazing. In 1890 the Haugh was let to the carter James Hamilton of Northgate at £8.10/-, for his horses. The newly planted trees, which still flourish, suggest the photograph dates from 1900.

The opening of the Bandstand on Ninian's Haugh in the summer of 1901, the planting of trees on the river bank and the laying of footpaths, transformed a sheep grazing meadow into a public park. The work was completed in the summer of 1908 when the council erected four swings, four see-saws, a maypole and a sand hole for children. Within weeks the problem of boys monopolising the swings, and leaving out the girls, was tackled with a notice reserving two of the swings for the young ladies, and a park ranger, who also looked after the burgh's bowling greens and curling rinks was employed to enforce their ruling. Overshadowing the park is the five span Tweed Bridge which in 1897-1900 was widened to 40ft from its 1834 width of 21ft. To finance this, the Police Commissioners borrowed £8,000 from the Airdrie Savings Bank, repayable over 50 years at a rate of 3¼%.

Willie Mackey (perhaps fifth from left) and his Pierrots – including the Mansen Sisters, Mimi and Maudie, the *Dainty Duettists and Dancers* – on Ninian's Haugh bandstand for his second season, in 1911. A little difficulty arose at the town council meeting on 14th August, when the Buildings Committee recommended that on wet evenings the troupe be given the Chambers' Town Hall at the reduced rate of 15/- per night. Treasurer Wilkie opposed the reduction from one guinea, not seeing why the Pierrots should get a reduction when others, connected with the town, did not. In fact, he would rather not see the Pierrots in the town at all. On a vote, the reduction was granted, by nine votes to two. The word 'Pierrot', derived from the sad, white faced clown, in white blouse and pantaloons, of 17th century Paris, but by the late 19th century had come to mean a concert party.

An 1880s photograph from the south bank of the Tweed with the bridge and the parish church on Castlehill. When the Rev William Dalgleish (1734-1807) was appointed to Peebles in 1760, his church was the 13th century Cross Kirk which, having been the parish church since 1560, was close to the state of ruin in which it still stands on Cross Road. Architecturally, the new 1784 built church was not a success. In his submission for the *New Statistical Account* for Peebles (1845), the Rev John Elliot writes; *It is a substantial edifice ... and if a little more architectural taste had been shown, it would have been very ornamental to the High Street. The massive steeple which, by being built inside the church, destroys the uniformity of the gallery, should have been placed outside of the church, and flanked with a few pillars. The seats in the body of the church, by running across instead of lengthwise, make the audience sit with their side to the pulpit.* The Ordnance Survey Name Book of 1856 reports that it seated 800, with an average attendance of 550. However, by 1887 it was gone.

Tweed Green, from the Tweed Bridge in 1905, with the five arch ramp leading down from Port Brae, in the foreground. Rising behind, are the buildings on the south side of High Street, ending with the spire of the Leckie Memorial Church (later St. Andrews Leckie Parish Church). Over the years, the two whitewashed cottages have each had a storey added; the building with the loft door is now a dwellinghouse, The long building, fronted by the joiner and upholsterer, John Grieve, was owned by the draper, William Melrose and let to the Peebles branch of the YWCA. Melrose's shop in High Street is now (2022) occupied by William Purves, Funeral Director.

A 1906 photograph, looking up Portbrae from the bridge, with the Parish Church overshadowing the Tweedside Inn (2022, The Bridge Inn). To the right, on the High Street corner, with its Italianate tower was the house of William Buchan (uncle of author John Buchan, *The Thirty-Nine Steps*), who was manager of the adjacent Commercial Bank of Scotland. What would become the Tweedside Inn, gets its first press mention in the *Peebles Advertiser* in April 1860; *Through the enterprise of Mr Archibald Donaldson, a comparatively worthless house, at this end of Tweed Bridge has been pulled down, and preparations are in progress to erect neat modern shops on the site*. One of the shops was taken by the baker, James Mitchell – who lived above the shop – who, around 1874, was succeeded by the public house keeper, George Brown who opened the Tweedside Inn. With plans for the widening of the Tweed Bridge advancing, the town council bought the Tweedside in 1899 for £1,600, demolished it, and had today's building completed by 1905 at a cost of £2,000, which they leased to the East of Scotland Public-House Trust.

A gathering of the Ancient Order of Foresters, probably the local branch Court Neidpath No. 5949, on Tweed Green in 1904. Founded in 1874 they met, at this time, in the Good Templars Hall on School Brae. It assisted members in times of hardship through sickness and death – by their 50th anniversary this branch had paid out £4,150 in sickness benefits and £990 in funeral costs. On the left of School Brae junction was the Burgh School, with the Grammar School to the right and the roof and spire of the 1875-76 built Leckie Memorial Church reaching above.

Tweedside Mill, with the parish church towering over it, photographed from the south bank of the Tweed, at the Minister's Pool, in 1924. The Ordnance Survey Name Book, published in 1858, describes it as; *A ruin at the west end of the High Street, and south of Castle Hill it was the Corn Mill belonging to the Burgh, but got burned down a dozen years ago. It is now let to a person* [Thomas Dickson] *for the purpose of making it into a Woollen Factory.* In January 1857 the town council advertised it for let as a water-powered waulk-mill (the process of thickening cloth by soaking and beating) and was taken by the Hawick woollen merchants Laing & Irvine, on a 19 year lease, for £800. In 1875 Alexander Laing and William Irvine were bankrupted and Tweedside, to which they had made extensive improvements, was sold to Walter Thorburn & Bros. for £9,000.

A 1921 aerial photograph of the town from the east, centred on March Street Mills, flanked by March Street on the left and George Street to the right, as they run to Rosetta Road.

March Street from the Rosetta Road junction, looking to the wooded slopes of Ven Law, with Andrew Burnett's grocer's shop on the left. At the planning stage of Messrs David Ballantyne & Co.'s mill on a greenfield site in 1884, the town council feued the land surrounding it for housing on Rosetta Road, and the newly-formed George Street and March Street. The Peebles' builder William Tod, and David Nimmo the joiner, bought many of the plots and by the following summer had built detached and semi-detached cottages.

A tartan dressed lorry, with a hand loom and bagpiper, within March Street Mill. Above the tailgate, which bears Peebles' coat of arms, a board proclaims 'Peebles for Pleesure and the Budget [Protest]' dating it to September 1909 when it was driven to King's Park, Edinburgh to join a crowd of 20,000 organised by the Budget Protest League. A nation wide movement, formed in June that year, it opposed David Lloyd George's 'Peoples Budget' which, to finance the Old Age Pension, brought rises in income tax, increased death duties and raised the tax on alcohol and tobacco. One poster proclaimed; *Less Beer – Less Baccy – Less Employment – and – They Call This the People's Budget!*

The entrance to March Street Mills festooned for the 1909 Beltane Festival. In March 1884, when Peebles' Police Commissioners granted permission to David Ballantyne (1827-1912) of Walkerburn to build a tweed mill *in a field between the old Railway Station and Rosetta Road*, he engaged the builder Messrs Herbertson & Sons of Galashiels. Work on the lodge, to the right in the photograph, was started immediately by Robert Mathison, builder, Miller Street, Innerleithen and in May 1884, Adam Dalgleish, the mill's first mechanic, and his wife Alexandrina moved in. By the following February the land on March Street, Rosetta Road and George Street, had been feued for housing.

The North British Railway station, Peebles East, at the end of Dean Park around 1910, when the house at 2 Dean Park, on the left, was owned by Margaret Kerr Fraser, wife of William D B Fraser of the Cross Keys Hotel, Northgate. The Peebles Railway Company was founded at a meeting in the Tontine Hotel, Peebles on Tuesday, 13th April 1852, with plans to raise £80,000 (8,000 shares at £10 each) to build an 18 ¾ mile, single line railway between the town and Eskbank (Dalkeith), where it would join the North British Railway line to Edinburgh. The first sod was cut at Peebles on Monday, 8th August 1853 and the railway contractor Bray & Dyson of Leeds had the line completed for its opening on 4th July 1855. Initially there were six services per day; 8.00am, 11.00am and 5.00pm from Waverley Bridge, Edinburgh, and 7.30am, 10.25am and 4.15pm from Peebles, In its first year it carried 7,504 tons of goods and 115,966 passengers. In September 1861 the line and station was leased to the North British Railway.

Edderston Road, running south, from Caledonian Road around 1906. The houses on the right, 3 and 5 Edderston Road, 'Burnside' and 'Strathnairn' (initially named Brooklyn Villa), date from the late 1890s and probably built by Dickson & Clyde, having finished the West Church. With accommodation variants over the years, the houses contained '2 Public-Rooms, 3 Bedrooms, Bed-closet, Bathroom (h & c), Kitchen, Scullery, Servants Room and other Conveniences'. Seven semi-detached houses had been completed by 1906. It was named after the Edderston Burn and followed its course as far as Tantah Croft, with further developments in later years.

The view across the town from the golf course in the 1930s, with the old clubhouse on the left and St. Andrews Cemetery, at the end of Wemyss Place, to the right.

Peebles Golf Club's clubhouse at Kirklands, around 1914, with the course extending to the left, and the house 'Yomah' (now 38 Kirkland Street), to the right. When founded in 1892, the 166 members played over a nine hole course on Edderston Farm's Morning Hill, leased from the Earl of Wemyss and March. In May 1908 it moved to Kirklands, where an 18 hole course was laid out. The clubhouse, with accommodation for the clubmaster in the loft space, was built at a cost of £761.5.5, and served until 1996 when the present clubhouse opened, and it was demolished, becoming part of the car park

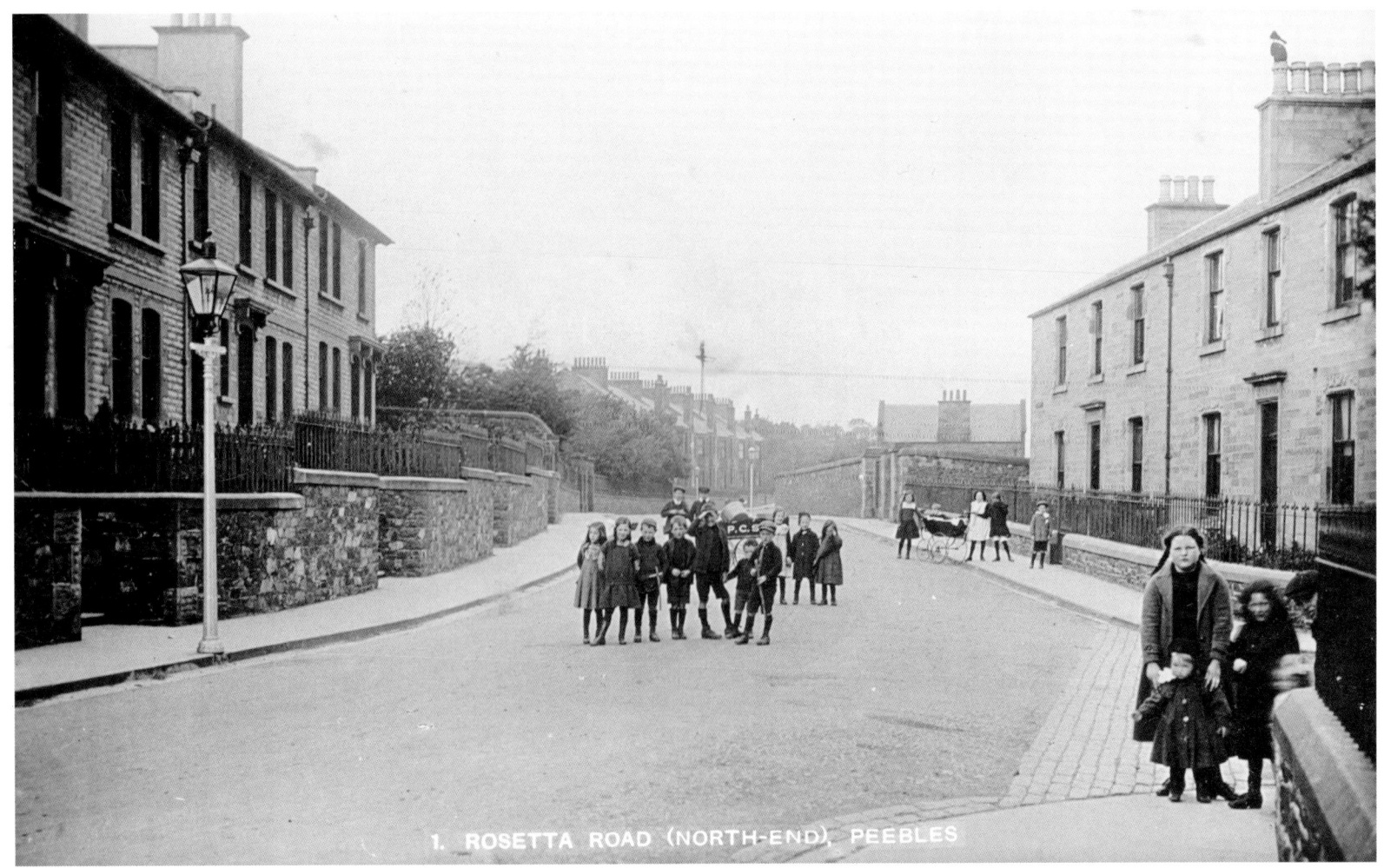

1. ROSETTA ROAD (NORTH-END), PEEBLES

Rosetta Road, looking north from the George Street junction, in 1913. On the right, before the Combination Poorhouse, is the semi-detached house (66 – 68 Rosetta Road) built in the mid-1890s by the architect and builder George Wilkie who succeeded his father, also George, who had died in 1892. Wilkie also built the terrace (57-67 Rosetta Road) on the left. The family appears on the 1841 Census living in Northgate, with George (senior) a 20 year mason, moving to Hayfield, 1 Damdale in the late 1870s. George (junior) was active in the town council, serving as treasurer and magistrate, and at his death in January 1922, aged 68 years, was Provost.

The Early Gothic style St. Joseph's Church on Rosetta Road photographed from Wemyss Place, before today's need for car parking. Prior to its opening, in December 1858, the clergyman, The Rev James Clapperton (1813-1901) alternated his services between Traquair House Chapel and a house in High Street, rented from James Turnbull by the Earl of Traquair, and fitted up as a chapel. St. Joseph's was blessed, on Wednesday, 29th December 1858, by Bishop James Gillis (1802-1864), Vicar Apostolic of the Eastern District of Scotland. The day's celebration ended at the Tontine Hotel with the clergy, choir and congregation as guests of the Earl of Traquair. The Rev. Clapperton retired from his Peebles charge in 1883, was conferred the title Monsignor in 1899, and died at Fochabers, Moray, in July 1901 in his 88th year.

Rosetta Road in the early 20th century, looking north from the Wemyss Place junction. The name comes from Rosetta Estate, purchased as 'Acrefield' in 1807 by Thomas Young (1753-1836), a military surgeon, who accompanied Sir Ralph Abercrombie's 1801 Egyptian expedition, when the Rosetta Stone was taken from the French and brought to Britain for display at the British Museum.

A burnt-out pavilion of the Peeblesshire Fever Hospital on Rosetta Road after a major fire on the evening of Thursday, 8th July 1909. When the alarm was raised at 6.30pm, Peebles Fire Brigade and the brigade from March Street Mills attended and extinguished the fire. Opened in 1895, when scarlet fever, typhoid and diphtheria were common diseases, the three pavilion, 20 bed hospital was built of corrugated iron on a brick foundation, at a cost of £1,800. Following the fire, the £1,600 re-build was completed in December, and patients returned from the Combination Poorhouse, opposite. The Fever Hospital was later converted to a geriatric hospital, and served until 1984. In 1987, with the site cleared, Hanover (Scotland) Housing Association built 35 one and two bedroomed flats with factoring service, in what is now Rose Park.

The entry to Eliot's Park, from Rosetta Road in autumn 1922. James Watson, the tenant of Eliot's Park Farm died in September 1919 and, encouraged by Lloyd George's 'Homes Fit for Heroes' scheme, Peebles Burgh Council bought part of the farm's land from its proprietor, Harry Charles Eliot, for housing. Work on building the 64 houses in Eliot's Park started before the year ended, but was stopped in January 1920, when Mr W H Swanson, the clerk of works, found the bricks unfitted for house-building. Only 50 of the 64 houses were completed, each costing £1,150 to £1,250 each. In January 1924 some of the houses were being offered for sale, and No. 4 was bought by a Mrs Mabel J Johnstone.

The memorial gable to George Meikle Kemp (1795-1844) at Redscaurhead (Moy Hall) on the Edinburgh road, north of Peebles. The work of James Grieve (1863-1939), an architect / clerk of works, it was unveiled by Kemp's daughter-in-law Mrs William George Kemp, on Saturday, 1st October 1932. Born at Hillrigs Farm, north west of Biggar in 1795, Kemp served a four year apprenticeship here, as a carpenter and wheelwright, with Andrew Wright until 1813, when he left for Galashiels. Tradition has it that on his walk to Galashiels he was given a 'lift', part of the way, on Sir Walter Scott's carriage and pair. He continued his work as a carpenter, whilst studying architecture, visiting cathedrals in the south of England and France. By the early 1830s he was with the Edinburgh architect William Burn, and in 1836 entered the competition for the design of the Scott Monument on Edinburgh's Princes Street. He came third. However, the committee decided on a second competition – which he won. The foundation stone of the 200 feet high monument was laid in August 1840 and under his supervision, work began in 1841. Kemp would not see its completion in autumn 1844. On the evening of 6th March whilst returning to his home in Morningside from a meeting with David Lind (1797-1856), the contractor of the monument, and on the pathway along the Union Canal near Fountainbridge, he fell into the water and drowned. His body was not found until Monday, 25th March.

Alexander Fairbairn (1845-1929) with his wife Jane née Tod (1855-1939), married at Colinton in 1874, seated on a bench outside their home, Redscaurhead Cottage, in the early 1900s. Alexander was a shepherd with Andrew Pringle Cairns of Eshiels, and tenanted the cottage between 1894 and 1919. Being on the roadside, and with a little enterprise, Jane opened her house to walkers and cyclists for refreshments and became a favourite 'Old Howf' for St. George's Cycling Club of Edinburgh. Taking the train to Peebles, club members cycled to Redscaurhead, where they were attended to by the 'Lady of the Manor'. For the couple's golden wedding anniversary, in July 1924, the club presented them with two handsome easy chairs at their new home at 1 Smallholding, Burnfoot, where Alexander died in 1929, aged 84 years. Jane passed away at the same age, a decade later. The sign on the wall, by the window, reads; Refreshments – Potass (an aerated water containing potassium bicarbonate) & Milk.

Left: Twelve year old William James Scott dressed as a pierrot for the 1913 Beltane Festival, when Miss Dora Kerr of Priorswood Villa, and dux of Kingsland School, was queen. The son of Kincardine born Robert Douglas Scott, living at 33 Crossland Crescent, who, with his twin brother James Mitchell Scott, ran Scott Brothers, the ironmongers, at 48 High Street. William joined the business and in September 1931, married Agnes Anne Hogg at the Old Parish Church. He died at Peebles in 1987.

Right: Forty-three year old Bandsman Robert Hume – and his tuba – of the 3/9th Royal Scots at Kingsmeadows Camp, Peebles, in May 1916. A power loom tuner, he lived at 27 Leithen Road, Innerleithen with his wife Margaret Ann, née Mitchell and their three children. Having been treasurer to the Innerleithen branch of the Pleasant Sunday Afternoon movement, *and a great help in the orchestra*, he was presented with a smokers companion and tobacco pouch, when he enlisted with the Royal Scots in February 1916. He died at Viewfield Nursing Home, Selkirk in June 1948.

Caverhill House in 1913, when it was Manor Valley Sanatorium, a hospital for the treatment of Tuberculosis (Consumption). In 1901, Dr Thomas Francis Spittal Caverhill, no relation, (1855-1910) of Edinburgh, an expert on Consumption having, in 1898, published an article in the *British Medical Journal*, *The Open-air Treatment of Consumption*, rented the house and 20 acres of land from the Earl of Wemyss – and purchased it in 1905. He built a wooden seven bed pavilion, a chalet with four beds and a cottage with three, with a spray bath for every two rooms. In 1917 it had 33 patients, but was empty by 1940 when requisitioned by the War Department as a storage depot. Between the late 1940s and the late 1950s, Angus Murray Cameron (1898-1969) ran it as a restaurant serving up to 1,500 lunches and teas, over weekends, to bus tours. It is now in private ownership.

An Andrew Harper REO charabanc on a tour through Peeblesshire in the late 1920s. Built by Ransom Eli Olds of the REO Motor Car Company, Lansing, Michigan, USA, the chassis were shipped, leaving the bodywork style to customer choice. Harper came to Peebles from Broxburn, where he ran a road haulier's business, in 1923, renting the house at 23 Eliot's Park (No. 64 from 1924) and a yard on George Street – and changed from goods carriage to passenger transport. In April 1923 he opened the first bus service between Peebles and Walkerburn, with seven journeys daily. His expanding service network embraced Edinburgh, Biggar and Dumfries, and by his retiral in 1936, when he sold out to the Caledonian Omnibus Company, he had a fleet of 27 buses. He and his wife Lizzie née Morris, moved to Edinburgh, where he died in February 1943.

A 1912 photograph of the east facing front of Kingswood House looking onto what is now Kingsmuir Drive, from where it is now accessed. With four public rooms and seven bedrooms, it was built in the early 1860s as a summer retreat for Huntly born James Roy (1817-1881), a lace merchant, of 10 Arniston Place, Edinburgh. At the original entry on Bonnington Road were the stables, with servants and gardeners accommodation. Between 1882 and 1902, Robert Langford Dalzell Cannon (1847-1911), and his wife Diana Langford Cannon née Norman (1831-1897) of Albert Gate Mansions, Knightsbridge, London, spent their summers here, leaving their initials – RLDC – DLC – on the lintel of an upper storey window.

The south west facing front of Kailzie House and the bridge over the Kailzie Burn around 1900 with, perhaps, James Adam, Lord Adam (1824-1914), a Senator of the College of Justice, and his wife Catherine, who tenanted the estate from the trustees of William Connel Black, who had died in 1895. Kailzie is named in the *Laws and Acts made in the First Parliament of Our most High and Dread SOVERAIN, JAMES VII, by the Grace of God, King of Scotland, England, France and Ireland. Holden at Edinburgh, the Twenty Third day of April 1685. In A Proclamation for calling together the Militia on this side of the Tay (p.145), appear the names John Balfour, Sheriff-Deput of Kailzie and William Burnet of Kailzie.* The *Caledonian Mercury* of Thursday, 9th February 1749, carries the following advertisement, offering the house for rent; *The MANSION HOUSE of KAILZIE, within one Mile of Peebles, and seventeen miles of Edinburgh: The House pleasantly situated upon the River Tweed, containing twelve Fire-rooms and a great many Closets, a good Kitchen, Brewhouse and Cellars, with large and convenient Stables, Granaries &c. and also two Gardens, a Bowling Green and a Pigeon-house, contiguous thereto.* It passed through a number of owners before being demolished in 1958.

Scots Mill on the south bank of the Tweed, two miles east of Peebles on the Cardrona road (B7062), around 1904, when owned by Florance William Black of Kailzie. The mill still stands between the road and the river with the miller's house across the road opposite. Built of whinstone rubble, it has a stone bearing the inscription – RNC.1802.SM – for Robert Nutter Campbell of Kailzie and, perhaps, Scots Mill. Having bought the estate in 1794, Campbell built a new mansion house, and ancillary buildings including this one as a saw mill and corn mill. The name *Scotsmill* features on William Roy's Military Survey of Scotland (1747 – 1755), but the identity of the miller 'Scot' is lost.

Priorsford Footbridge photographed in 1923 from Ninian's Haugh, on the right bank of the Tweed, with Priorsford Villa on the north side, and the 1860s railway bridge, carrying the Caledonian Railway line to Peebles (West) Station, beyond. The need for a pedestrian link between Tweed Green and the Springhill district, with Victoria Park, on the south bank was taken on by the town council, but financed by public subscription. In June 1904 a plan for the lattice girder suspension bridge was accepted from Robert John Mathison Inglis (1881-1962), a civil engineer with the North British Railway and son of the retired cotton merchant, James Inglis of Tantah House, Edderston Road. The bridge was built by Somervail & Co. of Dalmuir Iron Works, Clydebank, who also supplied the materials, and completed the work in 1906. In April 2021, Scottish Borders Council granted themselves planning permission to install new lighting and a handrail.

Between 1921 and 1939 Peebles Hydro Hotel, with its six grass and four hard tennis courts, hosted the Scottish Lowland Tennis Championship Tournament (later, the Scottish Grass Court Championships). Other venues between 1878 and 1994 included Edinburgh, Glasgow, Bridge of Allan, Moffat, St. Andrews and Wemyss Bay. This photograph dates to the early 1930s. The area held three bowling greens, until converted to tennis courts for the first championship event in 1921. Today (2022), it is a grassed area, with three hard tennis courts to the west (left). The stairway survives, but its flanking flower beds have not.

The front of 'new' Peebles Hydropathic Hotel, on Innerleithen Road, in the 1920s with two ladies, on the left, dressed as though coming from the tennis courts. The foundation stone of the original hotel was laid in August 1878 by William Chambers (1800-1883) of W & R Chambers, publisher, but due to a severe winter, the work of the architect, John Starforth, York Place, Edinburgh, was held up until March 1879, delaying the opening until July 1881. *The Scotsman* of 13th October 1881 carried the following advertisement; *The Peebles Hydropathic Establishment and Sanitorium. Charming situation, with fine southern exposure, Extensive Grounds; fine walks along Tweedside. Turkish and other Baths most complete. Public Rooms and Bed-Rooms unrivalled. Cheerful society … Lawn Tennis and Croquet Greens, with ample provision for thorough treatments of Invalids. Excellent Home for parties giving up housekeeping, or for Officers and others returning India, China etc. Terms 7s.6d. per day inclusive.* It was lost to an extensive fire on the evening of Friday, 7th July 1905, and at a cost of £70,000 re-opened in March 1907.

The Hydro's conservatory on the west side of the building, looking to the hotel building, a few days after the fire of July 1905. The 13ft wide corridor which ran 210ft through the centre of the hotel, continued a further 120ft as an iron and glass conservatory terminating with a 32ft diameter octagonal dome. It was preserved for the new building of 1907.

'Alex Burns and his Peebles Hydro Ambassadors', the Hydro's resident band between early 1930 and 1935. They first come to notice in *The Stage*, 'the British weekly newspaper of the entertainment industry', in June 1928, when playing at the Embassy Dance Palace, Manchester, followed by the Tower Oriental Lounge, Blackpool (August) and the Piccadilly Club, Glasgow until December 1929. Advertising accommodation (13/6 per day) for the Scotland v. Ireland, Rugby International Match at Murrayfield on 22nd February 1930 (Ireland's third successive victory at Murrayfield), the hotel had Alex and his band play for dinner dances on the Friday and Saturday evenings (7/6d). The last known of him was an entry in the personal column of *The Era* – The Official Organ of Entertainment – of 25th December 1935 – *Will Alex Burns (Bernstein), M.D., late of Peebles Hydro, Piccadilly Club, Glasgow, etc., or anyone knowing his whereabouts, communicate with Box 943, "The Era".*

On the south side of the Innerleithen road with two lodged entries, Kerfield House was built in 1800 for William Ker (Provost of Peebles 1773-1778), who died under its roof on 16th October 1807, aged 66 years. Divided to form two houses in the 1970s, the original house had three public rooms, seven bedrooms, two kitchens, servants accommodation, and a brewery. In the 1780s William spent time with a brewer in London, returning to establish Kerfield Brewery and produce 'Peebles Porter'. In 1810 the business was taken over by his son-in-law, William Aitchison, who had married his daughter, Mary Russell Ker at Peebles in 1804. By 1827, Aitchison & Co. was at 2 Infirmary Street, Edinburgh, but still producing 'Peebles Porter' at Kerfield, which sold at 5/- for a 3½ gallon cask or 3d per bottle.

The *Scots Magazine* of 1st September 1817 reported; 'Wire Bridge' – *Among the numerous objects of curiosity which attract the attention of strangers on the pastoral banks of the Tweed, there are few more worthy of notice than a wire bridge lately thrown over that river, at King's Meadows, about a mile below Peebles* by Sir John Hay, Baronet. This 1885 photograph, taken from the river's south bank, shows the bridge and Wire Bridge Cottage, when occupied by Thomas Douglas, and his family, a forester on Hay's estate. Built in 1817 by the Edinburgh iron merchant John Stevenson Brown (later Redpath Brown & Co.), for Sir John Hay (1755-1830) of Smithfield and Haystoun, the 110 ft span, 4 ft wide, bridge carried a pathway from the Innerleithen road to Sir John's 1795 built house at Kingsmeadows, on the south side of the river. It was removed in 1954 having been damaged by a tree brought down in a spate.

Royal Burgh of Peebles New Gas Works.

Estimated cost £20,000.   Opened 1st July 1905.

Peebles News Series

Peebles Corporation's Gas Works at Eshiels soon after its opening on Saturday, 1st July 1905 (the Hydro having burned down the previous week). Founded in the early 1840s, the Peebles Gas Light Company had a works, with two gasometers, at the west end of Castlehill, where the Eddleston Water meets the Tweed. In 1898 the corporation took over the works, as it was reaching its production capacity. Initially, gas had been produced for street lighting but between 1898 and 1902 consumption rose from 13.5 million cubic feet per annum to 24.5 million, due to increased street and domestic lighting, and 877 cooking appliances in the town. Built at a cost of £21.000, it stood on five acres of land feued from Haystoun Estate. The photograph, taken from the south, shows the railway track leading to the sheds (extant) where the coal was unloaded, the gas works with its chimney, and the gasometer. The two houses were occupied by the stokers, 50 year old Richard Harrity with his wife Janet and their 10 children, and 44 year old John Johnstone with his wife and five children. The introduction of natural gas in the early 1960s brought coal gas production to an end and the site is now a recycling centre.